Messages To Our Children

ALBERTA LAMPKINS

A.L. Savvy Publications
P.O. Box 30203
Clarksville, TN 37040
http://alsavvypublications.com

Copyright © 2014 by Alberta Lampkins

All rights reserved. This book may not be reproduced in whole or in part or transmitted in any form or by any means, electronic or mechanical, including photocopy, recording, or any information storage and retrieval system, without permission in writing from the publisher, A.L. Savvy Publications, P.O. Box 30203, Clarksville, TN 37040.

ISBN 13: 978-0-9903805-0-4
ISBN 13: 978-0-9903805-1-1 (eBook)

Cover design: A.L. Savvy Publications

A.L. Savvy Publications can bring Alberta Lampkins to your live event. For more information or to book an event, contact A.L. Savvy Publications at 931-257-8530 or email Alberta Lampkins at Alberta@alsavvypublications.com or visit the website at http://alsavvypublications.com.

To all the beautiful children in our world,
May you reach for the stars, follow your dreams and help to make a difference in the world!

Contents

Forward	Suzetta Perkins
Introduction Letter	Alberta Lampkins
Introduction	Alberta Lampkins

Jo Katherine Dessaw	1
Trudy Chaney	7
Clarence Chaney	11
Latrice Lauer	17
Marjorie Lucille Hairston	23
Mary Blythers Farmer	27
Suzetta M. Perkins	39
Laurise Laurent-Workman	49
Camille Williams	57
Ollie Williams	61
Nicole Keith	65
Marlon Keith	69
Chaplain Anthony Taylor	75
Simona R. Green	81
Shevelle Godwin	87
Lakesha Parker	93
Alisha Ndiaye	103
Benita Kay Hairston	105
Tracey Morrison	117
Brenda L. Brooks	127
Towanna L. Thomas	141
Dr. Valencia Warren-Gibbs (ABD)	149
Alberta Lampkins	155

Messages to Our Children

Forward

Messages to our Children is born out of love. Alberta Lampkins is a gentle lamb, whose giving spirit lends itself to the many causes for which she advocates in an effort to inspire life, love, friendship and kinship. She has paved the way for open and honest dialogue, as each contributor to this project provides an open window to human reality. Whether it is a poem, a collection of thoughts, or a letter addressed to a love one, *Messages to our Children* will make you reach into your own soul and take a long, overdue assessment of your own life's journey.

It is with great pride that I pen this message. Alberta Lampkins is a true friend, one I hold in high esteem. I value our kindred spirits as literary deliverers of the written word, and I wish her well in all of her endeavors and accomplishments.

If you take anything from the literary pieces found on the pages between the covers of this book, know that these are truths—the heart and soul of those who've shared their joy and pain, accomplishments and failures, and words of encouragement with the ones they love.

Suzetta Perkins
Author
Behind the Veil, A Love So Deep, Ex-Terminator: Life After Marriage,
Déjà vu, Nothing Stays the Same, Betrayed, At the End of the Day, In My Rearview Mirror

Introduction Letter

In the year 2005, my mother, Macieon Hairston, took ill and came to live with me in Fayetteville, North Carolina. Her health declined and she asked me to get her a composition book. She wanted to start writing messages to her grandchildren. I obliged her and got the notebook. However, before she could write a single word, we lost her on December 22, 2005. Her words went unwritten.

So, it is in her honor that I started this book project. May the words you have to say to your children, grandchildren, niece, nephew, godchildren or any child connected to you, never go unsaid or unwritten. May you find a moment to write your own message to your children.

I am humbled and truly grateful to each author who participated in this great project. Peace and many blessings to each of you and to all who read our words.

Alberta Lampkins
Project Coordinator

Messages to Our Children

Introduction

Every person has their own definition, thought or idea of what a family means to them. Merriam Webster defines a family as a group of related people including people who lived in the past. However, family means much more than just that. A family consists of people who share common values, goals, experiences, activities, hobbies, emotional and spiritual connections. These relationships are not always genetic.

Social connections and relationships come from many sources: friends, neighbors, teachers, military, co-workers, church family and much more. Any of these sources can be a valuable asset in our lives. Belonging to a group or a family gives us a sense of identity. It helps us understand who we are and feel part of something larger than ourselves. Social connections are in essence, a circle of support and important for everyone regardless of age or life stage.

A family at its best helps to bring about peace, joy, harmony, and strength to each other. In family, we find an abundant source of traditions, beliefs and values. People of all backgrounds, cultures and religion make up the foundations of a family. And though we all may be uniquely diverse, the common thread is that family is the strongest and most valuable time honored tradition.

The attachments are real, and when we bond together and embrace each other, we build and fortify relationships. The fellowship becomes the central source of socialization, cultivation, guidance and purpose. The nurturing of a family sustains us, and love, kindness, caring and concern for each other deeply roots us.

Messages to Our Children

As we evolve and grow, our values and the basic concept of family and connections should always remain ever-present. Family values should be treasured and nurtured for generations to come. We must create a foundation of guiding principles for our children, our nieces, our nephews, our god-children and all children connected to each of us. It is essential for our children to celebrate life and share in our hopes and dreams of a better tomorrow for them.

As we pass on the torch to our children and those connected to us, let us be the role models in whom they learn to grow and be successful. Let us be the guiding light for them to see respect, responsibility and love. Let us be supportive of each other and show a basic sense of oneness in uplifting family and in uplifting the world.

The vision of this book is to share

Messages to Our Children

our stories, our words, our family trees and our messages to our children and all the children connected to us. Our hope is that collectively, we may be a beacon of light to all those reading our words.

A message is simply defined as: a communication containing some information, news, advice, request or the like. This definition fits the purpose behind our expressions in *Messages to Our Children*. May our exchange of thoughts inspire our children to reach higher heights and empower them towards success!

Peace and many Blessings
Alberta Lampkins

Messages to Our Children

ACKNOWLEDGMENTS

A warm and hearty thank you to all the contributing authors, Jo Katerine Dessaw, Trudy Chaney, Clarence Chaney, Latrice Lauer, Marjorie Hairston, Mary Blythers Farmer, Suzetta Perkins, Laurise Laurent-Workman, Camille Williams, Ollie Williams, Nicole Keith, Marlon Keith, Chaplain Anthony Taylor, Simona R. Green, Shevelle Godwin, Lakesha Parker, Alisha Ndiaye, Benita Hairston, Tracey Morrison, Brenda L. Brooks, Towanna L. Thomas and Valencia Warren-Gibbs – without all of you, this project could not be as special as it has turned out!

Family isn't always blood. It's the people in your life who **want you** in theirs; the ones who **accept you** for who you are. The ones who would **do anything** to see you **smile** and who Love You no matter what.

-Author unknown

Jo Katherine Dessaw

LETTERS TO OUR CHILDREN

Recently, I overheard a small child ask his mother, "how are babies made?" Hopefully we all know the answer to that question, but the question caused me to think, how are parents made and what makes a good parent?

Carrying a child for nine months does not automatically make you a parent. A lot of parents are working from the theory of, "Everybody has to do what works for them." Of course this is true on a certain level. All we can do is our best. But what is our best and how do we achieve our best when it comes to parenting?

Being a good parent is one of the most difficult and challenging tasks on earth; it is a life time commitment and differs from child to child, even when they are raised in the same home. We as parents want only the best for our children. Parenting, like all important responsibilities in our lives, requires devotion, dedication and lots of preparation. Most of us will parent as we were parented, which is not always a bad thing. Many who disliked the way their parents parented, will often parent in the opposite way. Remember our parents were a product of their times and the cultural situations in which they were raised in. We have the opportunity to let go of any hard feelings and baggage we are carrying as a result of their parenting. We must let it go to improve ourselves as parents.

Parents must first be willing to accept the role and responsibilities that come with being a parent. Our life will not be the same, whether it is our first, and second or thirteenth child. Our time is no longer our own, as the little mini me's that live in our homes are now in charge and require our undivided attention and care, regardless of our plans or agenda.

Parenthood is a full time job and we as parents have the responsibility to model the behaviors in our lives we wish our children to imitate in theirs. These behaviors include the traits that will help the child to grow into productive, independent individuals. Qualities including, but not limited to, integrity, kindness, self-confidence, discipline, truthfulness and most importantly, love.

We must offer our children unconditional love above all else. But we cannot give what we do not have, so the first step to offering unconditional love to our children is to learn to love our self-first. Learning to love is an ongoing daily undertaking. The more we work on it the easier it becomes. Unconditional love does not require parents to be perfect. We will make mistakes, but we need to learn from our mistakes, and use the experience to help us become a better parent.

Being a good parent is a growth process for the parent as well as the child. There is no such thing as a perfect parent. So sit back, fasten your seat belt and enjoy the journey.

Remember dear children, you are our most precious gift and we love you. Forgive us, for sometimes we are confused with the job we have been given as your parent.

Messages to Our Children

Jo Katherine Dessaw is a native of Buffalo, New York, however, has been a resident of North Carolina for more than twenty years. She is the very pleased and proud mother of one fine young man.

Jo Katherine is a graduate of Canisius College in Buffalo, New York, where she earned a Bachelor of Science Degree in Accounting. Jo Katherine has served in the United States Army and recently retired as a Staff Development Specialist for County Government.

Jo Katherine is a Certified Spiritual Director and Master Catchist. She is active in various ministries with the Fort Bragg Catholic community. She is an enthusiastic reader and a proud member of the Sister Circle Book Club.

Messages to Our Children

"Every great dream begins with a dreamer. Always remember, you have within you the strength, the patience, and the passion to reach for the stars to change the world."

– Harriet Tubman

Messages to Our Children

Trudy Chaney

Family, I would like you all to know that the most important things in life are not material possessions, but they are those things you cannot hold in your hands. They are the things you hold in your heart, like love. No matter what happens in your life, love will always find a way to bring you back to a good place. Every day that we are here, we have an opportunity to show love and to be loved.

Love has so many different definitions and is described in lots of ways. One kind of love is, romantic love. However, a greater love, the love I am speaking about, is called Agape love. With Agape love we learn the true meaning of 1 Corinthians 13:4-7, which says: Love is patient, love is kind. It does not envy it does not boast, it is not proud. It does not dishonor others, it is not self-seeking, it is not easily angered, and it keeps no record of wrongs. Love does not delight in evil, but rejoices with the truth. Love always protects, always trusts, always hopes, and always perseveres.

Family I speak about love because most of my life I felt unloved, and it came out in so many different ways. Some good, but a lot not so good. I don't want you to waste time worrying about how someone else feels about you. I want you to focus on how you feel about yourself. If you love yourself, you will draw the right type of love to you. Again, I want you to know most of all that agape love is the love that no matter what will always be there. So, love God, love yourself and love each other.

Messages to Our Children

Trudy Chaney is the delightful wife of Clarence Chaney and mother of two outstanding sons, Al and Robert. She is also the proud grandmother of five wonderful grandchildren, Camille, Alexis, Ahmad, Lacharese and Connie. She has two beautiful great-granddaughters, Anyla and Summer Raine and one handsome great-grandson, Elijah.

Trudy holds an Associate's degree in Secretarial Science from Erie County Community College. She has been employed with M & T Bank for more twenty years – where she will be retiring from at the end of 2014.

Trudy is a native of Detroit, Michigan, however, has lived in Buffalo, New York for more than 40 years. She has been a loyal and dedicated member of Grace Tabernacle church, where she serves on the Usher board, for over twenty-year

Messages to Our Children

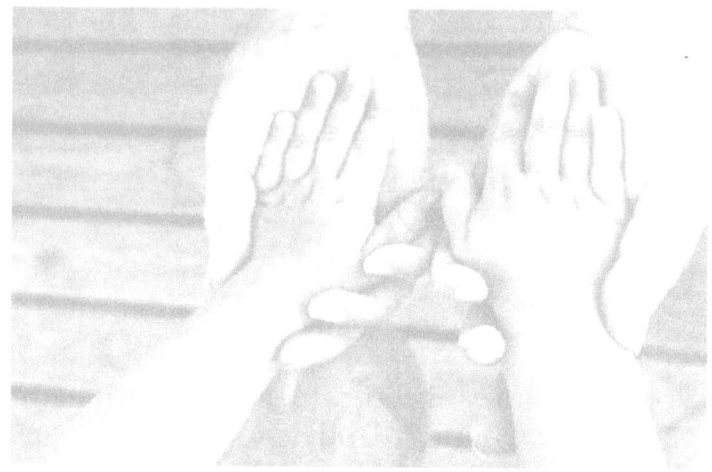

"Keep smiling because life is a beautiful thing. And there's so much to smile about."
-- Marilyn Monroe

Messages to Our Children

Clarence Chaney

I am a child of the 50's. I come from a very close family of six; four boys and two girls. Ruth Chaney, my mother, taught us how important it is to stick together. She would often tell us, "If one of you falls, it should be as if all of you have fallen." Her words resonate with me to this day and I have always done my best to keep my family standing. I started working in the 60's and worked various odd jobs, such as, cutting grass, trimming hedges, washing cars at the Texaco gas station and I worked as an apprentice butcher.

In 1968, I secured a job as a short order cook at a steakhouse and worked there until I enlisted in the United States Marine Corp. I proudly served my country as a Marine from 1972 to 1974. It is an experience that I will never forget. After my discharge from the marines, I worked at a steel plant from 1974 to 1980. Due to factories and other American businesses shutting down and moving overseas, I was laid off from the steel plant. It was a very rough time in my life. Work was scarce and I had a hard time finding a new job. The best thing about my life during that time was in 1979 when I met the love of my life, Trudy.

One day, during a cold winter, I was outside shoveling snow and my neighbor approached me. As we began to talk, I informed him that I was currently out of work and having a hard time finding a job. He encouraged me to apply for a position at the County Highway Department; he promised that he would put a good word in for me. I did just as he said and now, thirty years later, I am still employed with the County Highway Department.

Messages to Our Children

My relationship with Trudy stood strong and I was blessed with not only her in my life, but her two son's Al and Robert, who became my sons. Trudy and I have a great relationship and our family has grown. Alberta, our daughter-in-law, is very close to our heart, as if she was our own. The best thing is that we have five wonderful grandchildren, Camille, Alexis, Ahmad, Lacherese and Connie and three great grandchildren, Anyla, Summer Raine and Elijah.

From the 50's to now, I have had many joyous moments in my life. You never know the joy life has for you until you learn to just live. I have gained so much more than I could imagine. I shared my story and talked about my jobs because I want my family to know who I am and where I am in my life now. I want you all to know that you may start out one way, but there is always a surprise waiting for you. Live just for you. Working hard and having a great family has allowed me to grow in many ways and I count it all as "Joy." I wish you all the best in life and may each of you find joy.

Messages to Our Children

Clarence Chaney is the proud husband of Trudy and step-father of two wonderful sons, Al and Robert. He is the humble grandfather of five grandchildren, Camille, Alexis, Ahmad, Lacherese and Connie, two great granddaughters, Anyla and Summer Raine and one great-grandson, Elijah.

Clarence proudly served his country as a United States Marine. He has been an honest and hardworking employee with the Erie County Highway Department for more than thirty years.

Clarence is a native of Buffalo, New York where he resides with his wife Trudy and many other family members. He is an active and vital member of Grace Tabernacle Church. Clarence is a help to all those who know him!

Messages to Our Children

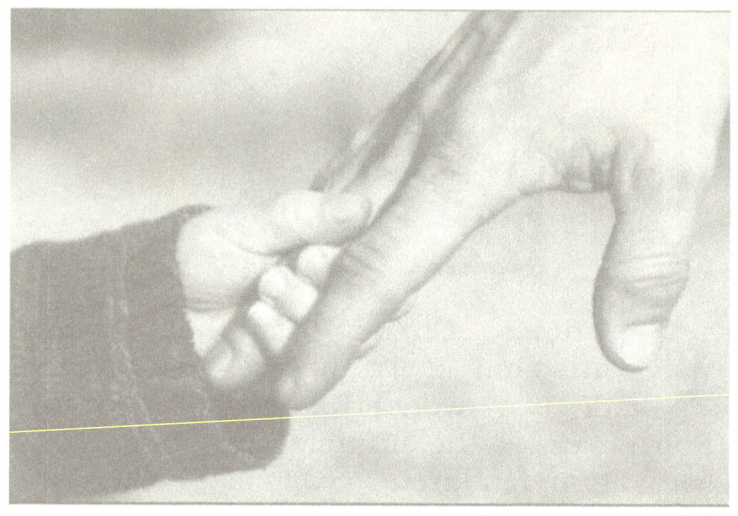

"To be a great champion you must believe you are the best. If you're not, pretend you are."

– Muhammad Ali

Messages to Our Children

Latrice Lauer

BROTHA OF BRONZE AND GOLD

I LOVE YOU BROTHA OF BRONZE AND GOLD

INTERNAL MYSTERIES WILL UNFOLD

STAND YOUR GROUND AND NOT BE TOLD,

YOU CAN'T ACHIEVE AND LOVE US BOLD.

THE CHILDREN OF NATIONS YOU WILL HOLD

I LOVE YOU BROTHA OF BRONZE AND GOLD

DRUGS AND GUNS YOU WILL NOT CARRY

A BEAUTIFUL BLACK PRINCESS YOU WILL MARRY

ON THIS EARTH YOU'LL ALWAYS TARRY

THE SWEETER THE JUICE, THE DARKER THE BERRY

Messages to Our Children

I LOVE YOU BROTHA OF BRONZE AND GOLD

YOUR MYSTERY WILL SOON UNFOLD

WORK ALL DAY, KOOLAID AT NIGHT

IN YOUR LADY YOU FIND DELIGHT

WORK EACH DAY WITH ALL YOUR MIGHT

WALKING TALL INTO THE LIGHT

YOU'RE NOT ABOUT THE STREETS WITH THUGS

YOU PREFER YOUR FAMILY AND PLENTY OF HUGS

ROYAL PRINCE AND KINGS YOU ARE

PRESSING FORWARD YOU WILL GO FAR

STANDING STRONG AND TAKING THE HEAT

WALKING WITH GOD YOU CAN'T BE BEAT

I LOVE YOU BROTHA OF BRONZE AND GOLD

THERE IS NO MYSTERY TO UNFOLD!

Messages to Our Children

Latrice Lauer is the beautiful mother of a lovely young lady, Ms. Shelby Lauer, whom she loves dearly. Latrice is also the daughter of a wonderful mother, Linda and granddaughter of a fantastic grandmother, Ruth Chaney.

Latrice is a hard working professional in the banking industry. She has worked in retail banking for more than fifteen years. She currently holds the title as a Senior Fraud Specialist.

Latrice is loved by everyone she meets. She has a bubbly personality that is infectious. She brings joy and smiles to all children and people connected with her. Latrice enjoys writing poetry, traveling and spending time with her family.

Messages to Our Children

Latrice is actively involved in the community and in her church. She has been a member of True Bethel for more than ten years. Latrice resides in Buffalo, New York with her daughter and family.

Messages to Our Children

Messages to Our Children

"You're braver than you believe, and stronger than you seem, and smarter than you think."

- A.A. Milne / Christopher Robin

Messages to Our Children

Marjorie Lucille Hairston

Here at age 53, as I look back over my life, there is nothing I would do differently. The lessons learned are priceless. Learning to pick your battles is key in maturing. Life will be hard, but it makes you stronger to be able to handle what's coming around the corner next.

There is no giving up or giving in, because the latter will be greater than the beginning. You will have more happy days than sad days. Always find a reason to laugh. Even if it is something goofy. Always hold your head high. Think about all the bad things our ancestors had to go through to get you where you are now.

Always keep GOD first. Always keep GOD close. Talk to him constantly. He

will never guide you wrong. Stay away from
Chaos. Stay peaceful. Run after peace and you will find her.

Messages to Our Children

Marjorie Hairston is the adoring mother of two fabulous young men, Curtis and Otis Jr. she is also the proud grandmother of her musically gifted grandson, Malachi. She is a native of Buffalo, New York, however has lived in the state of Maryland and North Carolina.

Marjorie holds an Associate Degree in Criminal Justice. She worked as a police officer for the Baltimore Police Department for over ten years. She left law enforcement and currently works in the medical career field.

Marjorie recently returned to her hometown of Buffalo, New York. In her words, "It feels good to be back home!"

Messages to Our Children

"Be Silly, Be Honest, Be Kind."
-- Ralph Waldo Emerson

Messages to Our Children

Mary Blythers Farmer

LIFE PRECIOUS GIFTS
TO MY CHILDREN
SCOTT A. FARMER, JR.
TIERRA JANAI FARMER

The first word that comes to my mind when I think of my children is BLESSED. I could never imagine all the joy my heart has felt by being a mother to my children. As I think back on my youth I believe I always wanted to have children. It was important to me to wait until I was ready to commit to this lifelong journey and to find the right husband to share this special gift with.

God first blessed me in September 1990 when I found out I was pregnant with my first child. After the initial shock wore off that I was indeed carrying a baby I loved my child with my whole heart and I wanted to be the best mom I could be.

Being I was raised by a single mother (Geraldine Rouse Blythers) after my dad (Benjamin Franklin Blythers, Jr.) passed away at such an early age (42). My mother truly loved her four children and she worked hard every day of her life to make sure we had all our needs met. By the example I saw by my mother and paternal grandmother (Ellen Nora Pickett). I felt I had a great road map to follow.

On April 10, 1991 my healthy baby boy (Scott Jr.) was born (7lbs 4oz). I really cannot put into words what that moment felt like, seeing him for the first time and knowing God had entrusted me to be his mother. My heart was filled with the joy only God can give a person. I often say children do not come into this world with instructions.

Messages to Our Children

As a mother I felt I would be fine, I would have to figure things out as I went along and that I did. With my first child, it was truly trial and error and after a while I got the swing of it. To have this little person who depended on me for their whole existence could have really been overwhelming, but I can honestly say it was not overwhelming for me. I enjoyed it all, the good, the bad and the ugly!

As time moved forward I knew I wanted more children (original plan was to have a total of six). I always had this fantasy about planning my children; however, it never quite happened that way.

February 1994, approximately, I found out I was expecting my second child. At this time in my life a lot had happened. Things had changed from me wanting six healthy kids to finding out what the sex of this baby would be. I was praying for a healthy baby girl. I prayed if God blessed me with a healthy baby girl then the shop would truly be closed. An ultrasound confirmed I was having a girl and I was over the moon with happiness. I said a prayer of thanksgiving to God for giving me the desires of my heart.

On September 18, 1994, my baby girl (Janai) was born (6lbs 5oz based on the doctor's calculations she was two weeks early) based on God's time she was on time. Again, the joy only God gives is how I felt on that Sunday morning when she was born. Now I was blessed to have two special people who would be connected to me for the rest of my life. What more could you ask for in life. Though my future as a mother was unknown to me, my prayer then and now, continues to be God guide me in all I do as their mother.

There are so many fond memories I have with my children it would be hard to pick just one, but there is one that really stands out in my mind. It was on Mother's Day a few years ago and my son had a bowling tournament out of town. He asked me if I would be willing to go with him, along with his sister. I agreed because what better way to spend this special day than with the two people who made it possible for me to be a mother.

The conversation between my children and I has always come naturally, so on this day it was no different. As we traveled we talked about many different subjects. On our return trip my children told me they were unable to get me a Mother's Day card, so they took out a sheet of notebook paper and made me a card saying how much they loved me. To this day I have that card because I know it came from their hearts.

After they read the card to me my children started talking about different sayings that I would say to them over the years. I was amazed at how accurate they were. It was the funniest exchange to date I can remember between my children and I. I remember laughing so hard that my sides hurt. I totally lost it. It made me realize that my children really paid attention to detail.

In closing, I wanted to do this project so that my children would know how much I loved them now and before they ever existed in my life. I will continue to love and support them in all they do in this life. Every decision I have made in my life, as it related to them, was based on my heart and wanting the very best for them. When I did not have all the answers, my hope was that they knew I would be there for them now and always.

Parenting is not easy and I continue to learn in this process call life.

Messages to Our Children

You both are the heartbeat of my existence.

I Love You Both Dearly
Respectfully Submitted
Mary Blythers Farmer
Mother to the Best Children in the World

Messages to Our Children

Messages to Our Children

Mary Blythers Farmer is the proud daughter of the late Benjamin and Geraldine Blythers. She is a native of Wilmington, North Carolina, however, currently resides in Fayetteville, North Carolina with her wonderful husband Scott and their two dynamic children, Scott Jr. and Tierra Janai, to whom she dedicates her life.

Mary holds a Bachelor of Arts degree in Political Science and Public Administration from Fayetteville State University. Her professional career is in Human Service. She has been employed in County Government for over 19 years. She has also been a Hospice Volunteer for over 4 years.

Mary is an avid reader and the founder of Sister Circle Book Club, which she established in 2000.

Messages to Our Children

Mary and her family have been true and faithful members of Mt. Hebrew AME Zion Church for over twenty-five years.

Messages to Our Children

Messages to Our Children

"Do not bring people in your life who weighs you down. And trust your instincts ... good relationships feel good. They feel right. They don't hurt. They're not painful. That's not just with somebody you want to marry, but it's with the friends that you choose. It's with the people you surround yourselves with."

– Michelle Obama

Messages to Our Children

Suzetta M. Perkins

A LETTER TO MY GIRLS
A HEARTWARMING SALUTE FROM A MOTHER AND GRANDMOTHER

By

Suzetta M. Perkins

To my daughter, Teliza, and granddaughters, Samayya and Maliah,

We don't say often enough how we feel about one another, although our hearts know for sure. Being too busy or unconsciously neglectful is no excuse.

I can say with the utmost pride and respect how much you mean to me, Teliza. In your thirty-seven years of life, I have loved you with all of my being from the time you came from my womb as a beautiful baby girl with a head full of coal-black hair. I watched you through my motherly lens, with my chest puffed out, as you grew up and progressed through life from a spunky elementary kid into a vivacious teenager, then on to college where you obtained your degree in four years. And then you blossomed into this beautiful, wonderful woman who was blessed to find the most fantastic mate, my son-in-law, now with a family of your own.

With fond memories I recall times when we lived in Germany and I accompanied you and your classmates on a ski field trip. I remember you getting stuck at the top of a hill and you yelling for me to come and rescue you, even though I had I was afraid to come down the hill I was on. I remember you going to

London and spending all of your money on a blouse at Harrod's, the Queens store, and I fussed about it while you tried to tell me you were only emulating what I did when we had gone to London on an earlier trip. I remember us going to Italy—riding the gondolas in Venice, marching through the Coliseum in Rome, dancing at an Italian restaurant, and staring at the Leaning Tower of Pisa. We traipsed all over Europe having the time of our lives. Those are memories I will always cherish.

There were moments we shared that weren't so grand, but as I look back on them now, those were growing pains, life lessons to be taken into the next chapter...the next phase of your life...my life. You were rebellious, much like your mother. You had strong ideas and beliefs that were the polar opposite of mine. And when mother's guidance had fallen on deaf ears and you experienced a fall from grace, it was mother you came to...to make it all well.

I see so vividly the day you married the love of your life—you coming across the bridge in your beautiful, white gown. I remember how your dad's eyes lit up...how my eyes lit up, seeing our daughter walk down the aisle, heading toward a new threshold of life. It was a beautiful day.

You were now married to the military, and it took you away from me. Lock, stock, and barrel, you uprooted from the life you once knew and followed your husband to Hawaii, Alabama, Texas, Kansas, and Georgia. My heart was empty, but I knew this was your time to spread your wings and fly. This was the time that I realized more so than ever, that you were going to be all right.

You've always had a thirst for knowledge. However, I didn't know that you were the little researcher, one who would in all aspects of your life search for the truth of a matter so that you would be thoroughly apprised on everything that concerned you. I remember when you became pregnant with my first granddaughter, you came to visit, and we had to watch the "Baby" channel morning, noon, and night. I haven't forgotten the instructions you gave your father and me when it was time for you to deliver my granddaughter—how we were to conduct ourselves and what we could and couldn't say to the doctors. I'm smiling.

I now have two wonderful granddaughters, Samayya and Maliah. Teliza, you're a wonderful mother…so nurturing and maternal. My granddaughters are the joy of my life, as I know they're yours. It's so amazing to watch the cycle of life repeat itself.

Messages to Our Children

And to my granddaughters, Samayya and Maliah, keep the spark burning. Samayya, you've said that you want to be a doctor one day. Grandma will always be there to help you realize your dream, although, you've already been following in grandma's footsteps, winning all of those Excellence in Writing awards at your elementary school. And I haven't forgotten the Adventures of Grammy and Sammy—our book we wrote together. It will come to fruition. And, Maliah, your time is coming. Although you haven't said what you aspire to be in life, because it is too early in your life to know, however, I'm sure that you're going to be outstanding in whatever it is.

Our legacy will always be that we loved one another to the fullest. Our hearts are intertwined and no one can undo the tie that binds. You all are my wonderful creations from God, and always

Messages to Our Children

know that you're the gift that keeps on giving, the wind beneath my wings.

Messages to Our Children

Suzetta Perkins

A native of Oakland, California, Suzetta Perkins resides in Fayetteville, North Carolina. She has two grown children, Teliza and Gerald, and two granddaughters she adores.

Writing has always been in her blood. While a senior in high school, Suzetta realized her first published work in her high school yearbook, in which she was co-editor.

Suzetta penned her first novel, *Behind the Veil*, in 2000, and it was published in 2006. Since then, she has published eight more novels that include *A Love So Deep, Ex-Terminator: Life After Marriage, Déjà vu, Nothing Stays the Same, Betrayed, At the End of the Day, In My Rearview Mirror,* and *Silver Bullet,* which will be released April

2014. Suzetta is a contributing author of *My Soul to His Spirit,* an anthology that received the 2006 Fresh Voices Award and was featured in the 2005 issue of *Ebony* magazine. Besides writing, Suzetta's other passions are reading and scrapbooking.

Suzetta is the President and co-founder of the Sistahs Book Club, and she is Secretary of the University at Fayetteville State University, her alma mater.

Messages to Our Children

"Never be limited by other people's limited imaginations. If you adopt their attitudes, then the possibility won't exist because you'll have already shut it out...You can hear other people's wisdom, but you've got to re-evaluate the world for yourself."

- Mae Jemison

Messages to Our Children

Laurise Laurent-Workman

February 24, 2014

To my children CURTIS, ADRIANNA, ALEXANDRA and BABY-COMING!

When my dear friend approached me to participate in this project, I thought "W*ow, what an amazing opportunity to continue to express my undying love for you all.*" I am so thankful to God for that. Never forget that, I love you guys and nothing can ever change that. With that said, I have two things that I would like to share with you; in hopes that you will ponder upon these words and gain inspiration and aspirations for your life.

My first note to you is this: The one thing that will help you live a fulfilling life is to clearly understand that you were not placed on this earth haphazardly. There is a purpose for your presence here, therefore seek to find that. Analyze your talents, your gifts, the way you connect with others, the little things that make you smile, the actions that bring you joy and you will be able to <u>decipher</u> what your <u>purpose</u> or calling may be. My loves, LIVE LIFE PURPOSEFULLY! Understand that everything, I repeat, EVERYTHING you do has an impact on those around you.

Therefore, choose to <u>plant positivity</u> and you will <u>cultivate goodness.</u> And that, in the grand scheme of things, is worth more than gold, because it will lead you to a life of love, peace and happiness (it may sound cliché, but I assure you it's the truth). Also, forgive those who hurt you. It is important to rationalize others' behaviors to be able to look past any hurt inflicted upon you. Just know that they may have values that are different from yours, may have been raised in different cultures or surroundings. Therefore, these factors may account for the acts that cause your pain. It's alright to feel the pain and cry about whatever it is, in order to release the emotional burden. However, once the hurt is released, it is imperative to look at the situation with your positive glasses on.

Secondly, my babies, I want you to understand that there is a clear delineation between legacy and inheritance. My prayer is that I am able to leave you a legacy of caring for and loving others. I was very blessed that my grandmother, your great-grandma, Datura Antoine Moise instilled in me the importance of reaching out and caring for those less fortunate than myself. Her actions and words, in concert, illustrated that, we all have a responsibility to extend a helping hand to others.

Messages to Our Children

My loves, please recognize that it's not because you are better than those living in impoverished countries; it is by <u>grace</u>, that you are where you are in life. Your circumstances are different, not due to luck, not due to happenstance, not due to economic prowess, or whatever other factors the mind can conceive; but simply by the grace of God Almighty.

Therefore, before you leave this earth, <u>reach out</u> to others who may not have the same opportunities as yourself, and open a door for them. When you do, share with them the importance of reaching out to someone else in the same manner. That, my dears, is the essence of legacy. It is my belief that such a legacy differs from inheritance in a profound way.

The legacy of caring for/loving others will permeate who you are in such a defining way that, there will be fluidity between the essence of who you are as a caring/loving human and its manifestation in your actions and its reaffirmation in your words.

The beauty of it all is, your children, grandchildren and great-grandchildren will breathe, and live that legacy, therefore will duplicate it in their life. A legacy passed on as a love-in-motion, has the propensity to stand for generations to come. Whereas, an inheritance may be passed down from generation to generation, but its viability is determined by the recipients. My children remember this: Do not ever miss a chance to perfect your own humanity. I love you all.

Messages to Our Children

Messages to Our Children

M. Laurise Laurent-Workman was born in Haiti, raised in Montreal, Quebec – Canada. She is thankful to have travelled the world, spending years in places such as Pyeongtaek Korea, and Okinawa Japan, to name a few.

M. Laurise possesses a B.A. in Foreign Languages, with a French Specialization; a B.S. in Political Science, Global Studies concentration from Austin Peay State University; and a M.S. in International Relations from Troy University.

M. Laurise currently lives in Clarksville, TN with her husband and three children and works for the Department of Army, as a program manager. She loves to travel, teach Zumba, spending time with her family and giving back to her community.

Messages to Our Children

"Be yourself; everyone else is taken."

-Oscar Wilde

Messages to Our Children

Camille Williams

Prayers for my Daughters

Courtney - I have watched you grow from the little girl who I use to send to school with crooked parts in her hair, to a wonderful mother, wife sister and most of all, daughter. I never had a doubt that you would find your path in life because you were always and continue to be a planner.

I know that you are a grown woman, but as I tell your girls, you will always be my kid and I will forever be proud of the woman you have become. Shukran (thank you) for the gift of my four beautiful grand chicks and the best son in law (son) a mom could ask for.

Messages to Our Children

Alia - You are my miracle, all of the trouble I had bringing you safely into this world was worth the gift of such a wonderful, smart, gentle and charitable young lady. My prayer for you is for the world to know what a great person you are as you give them their sports highlights on ESPN.

I want you to continue to read, learn and explore the world around you. Your view of the world will shape who you are. Shukran (thank You) for allowing me to be your mother and shukran (thank you) for being my "superstar rock star daughter"

Messages to Our Children

Camille Williams is the elegant wife of Ollie and gracious mother of two fabulous daughters, Courtney and Alia. She is the proud grandmother of four beautiful girls, Kiara, Erin, Kyla and Makayla .

Camille holds a B.S. degree in Social Work and Human Services. She is an advocate for Child Development and has worked with children of all ages. She is actively involved with making sure her daughter Alia reaches higher heights, socially and educationally.

Camille is a native of Buffalo, New York, where she resides with her husband and daughter Alia. She pays honor to her mother, Marilyn Keith for paving the way.

Messages to Our Children

"Just don't give up what you're trying to do. Where there is love and inspiration, you can't go wrong."

– Ella Fitzgerald

Messages to Our Children

Ollie Williams

Message to my daughter Alia

From the day I met the cute little girl with the "dog ear" ponytails, you were my daughter. I have been given the gift of being your father and I don't take it lightly. My wish for you is that you continue to be the bright level headed young lady that we raised you to be. Follow your dreams, because I know that you will be just what you told me you wanted to be as a little girl; the best sports reporter in the country. Please know that I will always be your protector, provider and most of all - your Dad.

Messages to Our Children

Messages to Our Children

Ollie Williams is the diplomatic husband of Camille and honorable father to two lovely girls, Courtney and Alia. He is the lively grandfather of four enjoyable girls, Kiara, Erin, Kyla and Makayla.

Ollie is a graduate of the Firefighter Academy and has worked as a Buffalo Firefighter for 18 years. He currently holds the title of Lieutenant. Ollie also works with Erie County as a Security Officer part-time.

He is a native of Buffalo, New York, where he resides with his wife Camille and their daughter Alia. He pays honor to his mother, Elsa Williams for giving him superior guidance in his life.

Messages to Our Children

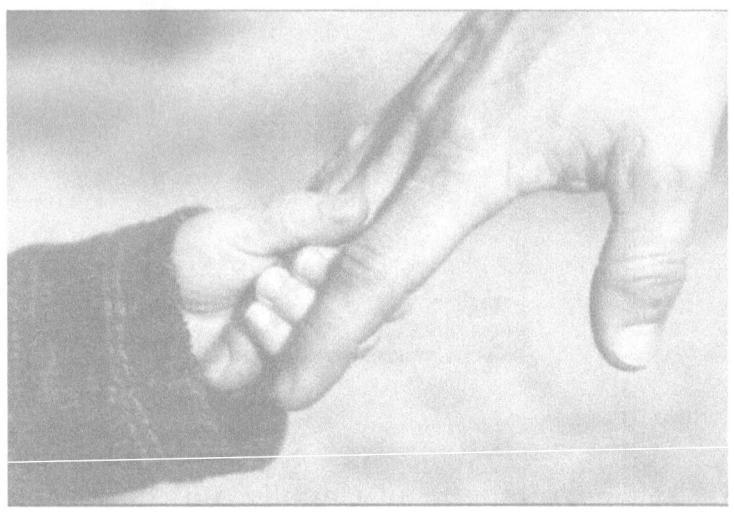

"It always seems impossible until it is done."

- Nelson Mandela

Messages to Our Children

Nicole Keith

Message to My Children

When I first looked into your eyes, I envisioned so much potential beyond the limitations of your circumstance. As a parent, I have always encouraged you to follow your dreams. Don't give up, hard work and determination does pay off.

I hope my life and the people I look up to serve as an inspiration. Yes there will be some ups and downs in this game we call life, but trust in God and he will direct your path. There is no right or wrong way to get your goals achieved. Be true to you.

Success is not measured by money

and accolades. Yes it's nice to have those things, but at the end of the day, those things don't always make someone happy. The love and survival of my family is what has been priceless to me.

You come from a rich ancestry and I would hope that those values are passed on to the next generations to come. You come from greatness, therefore you will be great.

Love
Nicole Keith

Messages to Our Children

Nicole Keith has been married to her magnificent husband Marlon for twenty-four years. She is the dynamic mother and step-mother of three fantastic children, Tiffany, Myles and Nicholas. Her parents, Bobby Earl Washington (RIP) and Inez Camille Washington Smith originate from Alabama; however, Nicole is a native of Buffalo, New York where she resides with her husband and children.

Nicole's professional career is in retail banking. She has been a full-time employee in the banking industry for eighteen years. She is a highly involved and dedicated member of True Bethel Baptist church. Nicole enjoys traveling and spending time with her family.

Messages to Our Children

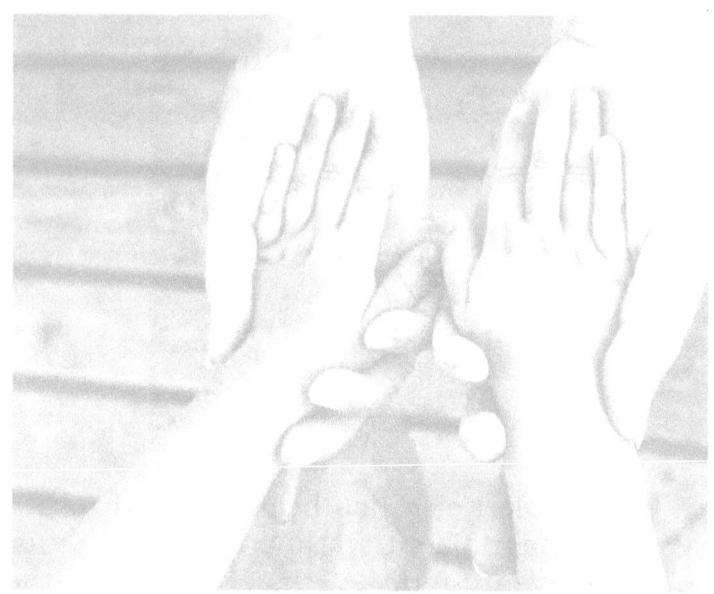

"Hold your head high, stick your chest out. You can make it. It gets dark sometimes, but morning comes. Keep hope alive. Don't you surrender! Suffering breeds character, character breeds faith. In the end faith will not disappoint."

~ Jesse Jackson, Keep Hope Alive

Messages to Our Children

Marlon Keith

To my children: Tiffany, Myles and Nicholas. All I ever wanted was to live long enough to watch you all become successful capable adults. Translated to be responsible adults who are prepared for all the good and bad things this world holds. Besides the almighty God, there is nothing and no one else more important to me, than you all.

I love you with every fiber in me and I pray that I have proven that while I'm yet on this side of glory. Please always remember to never be a follower of anyone else, well, other than Jesus. Learn to dance to the beat of your own drum and continue to make sound decisions.

Love Dad.

Messages to Our Children

Messages to Our Children

Marlon Keith has been married to his adorable wife, Nicole for twenty-four years. He is the proud and respected father of three super children, Tiffany, Miles and Nicholas.

Marlon's mother, Marilyn Keith originates from Alabama; however, Marlon is a native of Buffalo, New York, where he resides with his wife and children.

Marlon's professional career is in transportation. He has been a loyal and faithful employee with the Buffalo Niagara Frontier Transportation Department (NFTA) for more than fifteen years.

Marlon serves as a trusted Deacon at True Bethel Baptist Church. He also served as Chairman of the Deacon Board for a short time. Marlon enjoys vacationing with his wife Nicole, playing golf, target shooting and other outdoor adventures.

Messages to Our Children

Messages to Our Children

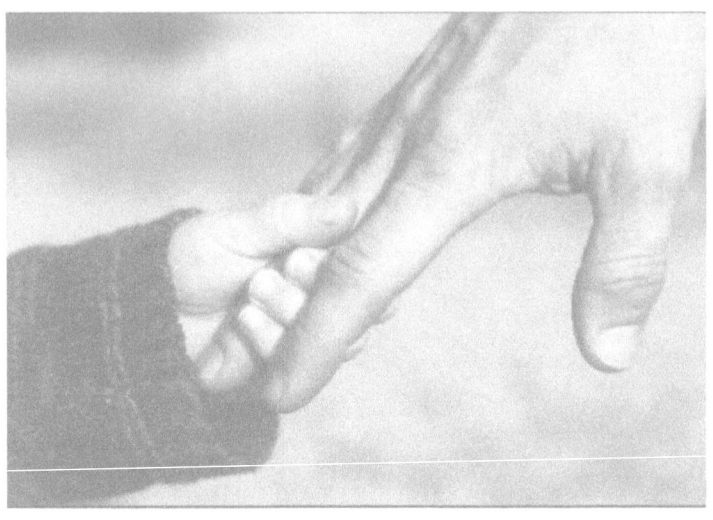

"Follow your dreams, they know the way."
- Unknown author

Messages to Our Children

Chaplain Anthony Taylor

Life Lesson

"Scarcity, the mother of all Inventions"

On an ordinary hill in a place called Moriah something extraordinary happened. Isaac, who was once bound and restricted, was set free. As a result Abraham named the place Jehovah Jireh. This became the mountain of provision. It was here that Abraham's faith was confirmed. God was moved by Abraham's unshakable, faith. "As it is written: "I have made you a father of many nations." He is our father in the sight of God, in whom he believed—the God who gives life to the dead and calls into being things that were not." (Rom. 4:17).

My faith was confirmed by God through my maternal grandmother, who understood how to make something out of nothing. She was an expert at making something out of nothing. I have fond memories of being in the kitchen with her on rainy days while she prepared good food. One of my favorite foods she prepared was glazed donuts made from canned biscuits.

During thunder storms she would say: **"Be quiet and let the good Lord do His work"**. So in great, but silent anticipation, I watched as she formed each biscuit in the shape of a small donut, slowly dropping them into a large deep cast iron skillet full of hot lard. When the cooked dough floated to the surface, it signified that they were ready. Then she would dip the hot crispy donut into a bowl of syrupy glaze made from a mixture of sugar and water. The final step was adding cinnamon to half the batch. The donuts were a true delight.

I also remember the sweet taste of snow cream she made only from the second wave of a snow storm. My grandmother would place one of her large cooking pots atop the awning to catch the snow. After retrieving the pot, she would immediately add sugar, canned milk, a pinch of salt and vanilla extract. It was the best snow cream in town.

From my grandmother, I learned a few things about cooking that have helped me to understand why I love good food on rainy days. However, the deeper lesson is what may appear to be insignificant to others, but significant to me. I witnessed how my grandmother was able to transform a can of biscuits into a sweet treat. She displayed love, not only through food, but through the miracle of her faith in God. Today I still believe in the power of God to make something out of nothing. "Jesus then took the loaves, gave thanks, and distributed to those who were seated as much as they wanted. He did the same with the fish. When they had all had enough to eat, he said to his disciples, "Gather the pieces that are left over. Let nothing be wasted", (John 6:11-12).

CH (MAJ) Anthony L. Taylor

101st Division Family Life Chaplain

Messages to Our Children

Anthony L. Taylor is a U.S. Army Chaplain and one of today's dynamic speakers on the themes of Faith development, spiritual resilience, empowerment, goal setting, marriage and family wellness. He previously served as senior pastor of a local church in Norfolk, Va. from 1992 to 2000.

Anthony holds a Master Divinity degree from Howard University, a Marriage and Family Therapy degree from Texas A&M Central, TX, a CPE Certification from Riverside Regional Medical Center and a Doctor of Ministry degree from United Theological Seminary. Anthony is the author of the book, *Irrational Faith*. Anthony and his wife, Paula are the parents of three adult children and resides in Texas.

Messages to Our Children

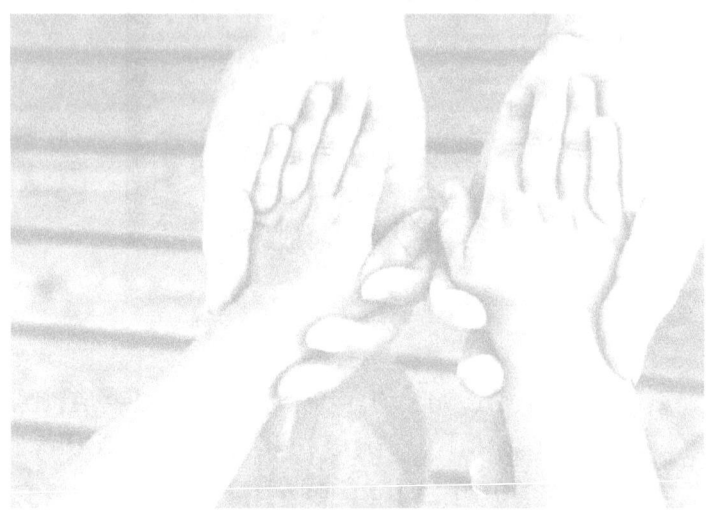

"In every conceivable manner, the family is the link to our past and bridge to our future."

-Alex Haley

Messages to Our Children

Simona R. Green

March 12, 2014

Dear Daughter,

I never thought a day like today would come, for me to see you and say the words, "My Daughter". I was not fortunate to experience bringing life into this world born through my canal. Providing stability, love and supporting your efforts in life doesn't require me to physically have given birth to you.

In today's society, you can be painted in a picture with different faces. You could have been a face of an abused soul, skin torn due to someone else's frustrations. You could have been a face of homelessness, surrounded in a world that doesn't show mercy, and care more for others that don't quite look like you and I. Instead you present a face to me, my dear daughter, of innocence and purity. You look to me for guidance and want of me to provide you with my love.

In my mind, I once believed it was required for me to have a natural birth before I could say that I am a mom. However, I have learned that is not true. You have brought to my life, joy, new life experiences and a sense of final accomplishment.

Everything I can share with you, I will, and everything I can do for you, I shall. I will do my best to right the wrong done to you in your life. You have completed me and made my family whole. On this day, dear daughter, I say to you, that there is no greater love than what we share.

Love you Always,
"Mom"

Messages to Our Children

Simona Renee (Davis) Green, resides in Raeford, North Carolina with her husband Ronald and their two toy poodles named "Chingy" and "Brooklyn." She is a military brat and a spouse of a military retiree.

Simona is a graduate of Fayetteville State University where she received a Bachelor's and Master's degree in Sociology. She has been employed with the United States Government for over fifteen years. She also does event planning and catering in her spear time.

Simona is a member of The Order of Eastern Star, Prince Hall Affiliation, where she provide service through such programs as the adopt the highway program, and working on various committees and projects in support of my surrounding community.

Simona will soon be the overly proud and joyous mother of an adoptive daughter or son.

Messages to Our Children

Messages to Our Children

Not flesh of my flesh.
Not bone of my bone. But still miraculously
my own.
And never forget for a minute.
You were not born under my heart.
You were born in my heart.

- Unknown

Messages to Our Children

Shevelle Godwin

To the children that I was never blessed to have from my womb, but was favored by God to have mothered them all with my soul. God has allowed me throughout the years to touch many with words, songs, or with simply a warm hug from my great big embrace. I have had lots of love to give and thank Heaven from above for giving me the heart from above to love so many with the true love that any mother can give.

Some think that you have to become a mother to know a mother's love, but look into the eyes of any little one or one in need and I will tell you differently. When you are willing to give your all and expect nothing in return and when you know what they need before a word is spoken. I can say I have been there; to a place of a mother's love without even having any little ones in my home, because I have been touched by a mother's heart.

Messages to Our Children

Shevelle Godwin is a native of Portsmouth, Virginia, however, currently resides in Fayetteville, North Carolina with her loving husband Robert and a host of family members to include fictive kin.

Shevelle holds a Master of Arts in Sociology and Bachelor of Arts in Sociology from Fayetteville State University.

Shevelle is an awesome and dedicated School Liaison Officer for Fort Bragg Army Installation and an Adjunct Professor of Sociology at Fayetteville State University. She has worked as a Social Worker and Day Care Coordinator for Cumberland County Department of Social Services.

Shevelle has received numerous awards: The Pete Taylor Award Recipient 2011,

2009, and 2008; 100 Best Communities for Fayetteville, 2011, and 2009; Pioneer Award; Recognized as Fayetteville State University Outstanding and Significant Adjunct Faculty in 1999; and several other community awards

Her Life Philosophy:
"My philosophy on life is ever evolving over time. One thing that doesn't change is ultimately we set the goal for the final delivery of our final life product. It has to be delivered ALWAYS with a goal of excellence that touches all areas of service every single day. My focus is to make sure that I have impacted someone in everything I do and do it as well it can possibly can. When we are at our best, we deliver something that is valuable, lively and interesting to another person's life."

Shevelle's Most Memorable Assignments:
"In serving our families and schools it's rewarding however I will never forget the call from the White House. The call came in from the East Wing seeing how schools work with families as they transition into NC and from other places all over the world. It's great to see that everyone is on board to assist families as they fight the war in other countries but we do what we

have to for them at home. In NC we do it with words and deeds."

Messages to Our Children

"Never give up on what you really want to do. The person with big dreams is more powerful than one with all the facts."
- Albert Einstein

Messages to Our Children

Lakesha Parker

To all three of my wonderful children, I have this to say... From the oldest to the youngest.

Dimone you are a parents dream. You are very good looking; clean cut, always neatly dressed, articulate and a very respectful young man. You are caring and always willing to give the shirt off your back if you had to. Keep those great qualities Dimone!

Latrice you are a very sweet, kind, outgoing, respectful, sentimental and nonchalant young lady. If you cry, Latrice will cry with you, without even knowing the reason why. Latrice, you have a special gift of compassion – don't ever let anyway change who you are!

Destiny you a very smooth young lady. You take whatever is being dealt to you and make the best of it. You are very smart, driven and determined. With all of your amazing qualities, I want you to know that *"the sky is the limit."* Go for it Destiny!

I am very proud of each of you. Continue to be the best at who you are and know that I will always love you!

Your mother,
Lakesha Parker

Messages to Our Children

Lakesha Parker is the fabulous mother of three wonderful children, Dimone, Latrice and Destiny. She will soon be the grandmother of a beautiful grandson or granddaughter. Lakesha comes from a large family of nine siblings; she is second to the last.

Lakesha has worked in the health care field and currently manages real estate property she owns. She is looking to invest in other properties.

Lakesha is a native of Buffalo, New York where she has resided her entire life. She enjoys spending time with her family and is known to bring laughter to the lives of all her friends. She pays honor and respect to her dearly departed mother, Orean Parker for being the source of inspiration in her life.

Messages to Our Children

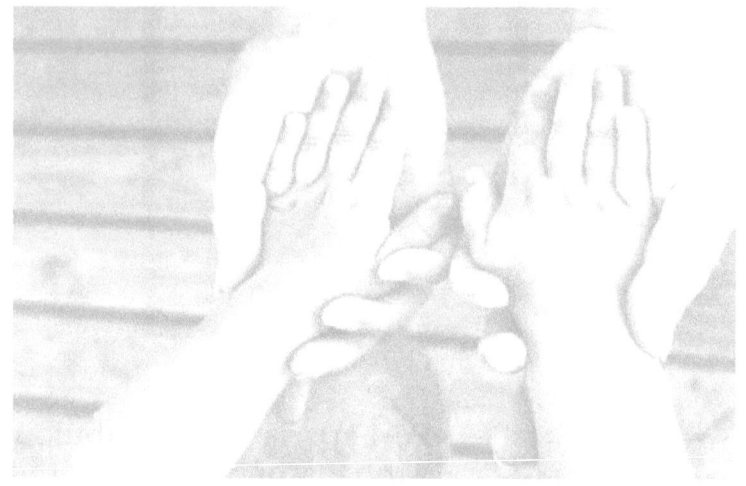

"Living in the moment means letting go of the past and not waiting for the future. It means living your life consciously, aware that each moment you breathe is a gift."

– Oprah Winfrey

Messages to Our Children

Alisha Ndiaye

To all four of my children

When I think back over my life, I realize that I didn't always make the best choices. Being a young mother pushed me to grow up faster than I expected. At times, I struggled, however, it was through those tough times that I found my strength and I found my purpose. God designed me specifically to be your mother. I admit, I am still growing and I am still learning how to be a good parent, but one thing is sure and that is, I will always try my best. I want each of you to know that you are capable of being the best at whatever you choose to do. I want you to always strive to be the greatest, finish school and go on to graduate from college. An education will give you more opportunities and help you reach higher heights. I am truly grateful to have each of you in my life.

Dashawn, my first born and my only son, I hope we always share the special bond we have. You are a big help to me and believe it or not, I learn from you every day. I hope you always know how special and smart you are. It is interesting how we both like animals. Because of your love for all kinds of pets, I believe that when you grow up, you will become a great Veterinarian.

Destiny, my first daughter. You are bright and beautiful and smart. You never hesitate to help out with your younger sister's and I appreciate you for that. Because of your love for helping others, I believe that when you grow up, you will become a great Teacher.

Eve, my sweet and caring daughter, you are a beautiful child. My life wouldn't be the same if I didn't hear your voice. From the moment you rise in the morning, to the time you fall asleep at night, you are talking. Because of your gift of chatter, I believe that when you grow up, you will become a great motivational speaker.

Majne, my beautiful daughter. My last, but certainly not least. You bring so much laughter to my life. I am amazed with how strong willed and independent you are. You seem to have no fear of life and are curious about everything. Because of your fearlessness and curiosity, I believe that when you grow up, you will become a great detective for law enforcement.

Messages to Our Children

Deshawn, Destiny, Eve and Majne, I know that your lives are only in my hands for a short time and I want most of all for each of you, is for you to be happy. Here is my prayer for you:

Dear Lord,
Watch over all four of my children
Be the eyes that see the things that I cannot see
Be the ears that hear the things that I cannot hear
Be the voice that speaks to them the words that I cannot speak
Allow them to grow and to learn and to be loved
Bless them to be the best at whatever you will have them to be
Protect their hearts
And
Cover me as I do my best to guide them.
Amen

Messages to Our Children

Alisha Ndiaye is the proud mother of four wonderful children, Dashawn, Destiny, Eve and Majne. She is a wonderful wife and a full-time employee with Wal-Mart.

Alisha is a native of Buffalo, New York, however, resides in Durham, North Carolina with her husband Abdul and their four children.

She is a natural lover of animals, enjoys the challenge of putting puzzles together, walking, spending time with her children and relaxing at home. She pays honor to her mother Benita Hairston for being her biggest supporter.

Messages to Our Children

"Don't expect your friend to be a perfect person. But, help your friend to become a perfect person. That is true friendship!"
- Mother Teresa

Messages to Our Children

Benita Kay Hairston

Note to my children/generations to come:

I Love you all and I am <u>very proud</u> of you. I am proud of all your accomplishments and how you are traveling on your life journey. I am very grateful to God that when the storms of life hit you, you have courage and willpower to bounce back.

I may not have been the best mother, I have made some mistakes, have some regrets, but I ask for your forgiveness. Learn from my mistakes and do better for your children.

To my grandchildren/generations to come: you have a very strong family line of intelligent, hardworking, successful people. Do your best, stick together and trust God to carry you through this life journey.

There are some things I have learned throughout my years of being here on earth that I want to pass on to you:

- Enjoy the life God has given you
- Don't cease praying and depending on God
- Don't depend on man, but trust God to work through man
- God sends blessings through people; God uses you to bless others and uses others to bless you
- The only thing you can do about the past is learn from it; so just look up and go forward
- I have witnessed and learned that God can do more damage to my enemies than I ever can; trust God to fight your battles

- One of my chosen sayings when things are not going as well as I desire is "Hold on, it's just a matter of time." God will bring you through difficult times in your life
- A smile and a hello will take you a long way

There is a saying which I find true about people and has helped me through life, so I pass it on:

If you are successful you will win some false friends and some true enemies – Succeed anyway

What you spend years building someone may destroy overnight – Build anyway

If you find serenity and happiness, they may be jealous – Be happy anyway

The good you do today, people will often forget tomorrow – Do good anyway

People are often unreasonable illogical and self-centered – Forgive them anyway

In the final analysis, it's all between you and God (it's was never between you and them anyway)

Finally, I will leave you all with a few scriptures which I keep dear to my heart:

Psalms 121:1-2 *I will lift up mine eyes unto the hills, from whence cometh my help. My help [cometh] from the LORD, which made heaven and earth* [this scripture became meaningful when someone tried to take my life and has carried me through the years]

Matthew 6:25-26 - *Therefore I tell you, do not worry about your life, what you will eat or drink; or about your body, what you will wear. Is not life more important than food, and the body more important than clothes? Look at the birds of the air; they do not sow or reap or store away in barns, and yet* *your heavenly Father feeds them. Are you not much more valuable than they?* [this scripture has kept me through my struggles]

Psalms 23:1 *The LORD [is] my shepherd; I shall not want* [this scripture has kept me through my struggles]

Psalms 46:1 - *God [is] our refuge and strength, a very present help in trouble* [this scripture helped through times of financial, career and legal trouble]

Hebrews 13:5 - *I will never leave thee, nor forsake thee* [this scripture provided courage when God was sending me into new territory]

Philippians 4:7 - *And the peace of God, which passeth all understanding, shall keep your hearts and minds through Christ*

Jesus [this scripture provided comfort when I was concerned about my children, my job and the storms of life]

Palms 37:23 *The steps of a good man are ordered by the LORD: and he delighteth in his way.* [this scripture helped me in my career and continual relocation]

Hebrews 11:1 *Now faith is the substance of things hoped for, the evidence of things not seen* [this scripture helped me through every aspect of my life]

Isaiah 40:31 *But they that wait upon the LORD shall renew their strength; they shall mount up with wings as eagles; they shall run, and not be weary; and they shall walk, and not faint* [this scripture helped me through the struggle, through the promotions, the success as well as overcoming my enemies]

Messages to Our Children

John 3:16 *For God so loved the world, that he gave his only begotten Son, that whosoever believeth in him should not perish, but have everlasting life.* [this scripture always reminded me of how much God loves me, regardless of my failures, disappointments, failing short of His glory and it also reminds me to love people the way God loves me]

2 Timothy 2:15 - *Study to show thyself approved unto God, a workman that needeth not to be ashamed, rightly dividing the word of truth* [this scripture is so meaningful in my calling]

Proverbs 4:7 - *Wisdom [is] the principal thing; [therefore] get wisdom: and with all thy getting get understanding* [this scripture reminds me to ask God for wisdom in everything I do]

Proverbs 3:5-6 *Trust in the LORD with all thine heart; and lean not unto thine own understanding. In all thy ways acknowledge him, and he shall direct thy paths* [this scripture reminds me to seek God for direction in every aspect of my life]

1 Peter 5:6 - *Humble yourselves therefore under the mighty hand of God, that he may exalt you in due time* [this scripture helps me as I acknowledge that I was born to lead]

Psalms 75:6-7 *For promotion cometh neither from the east, nor from the west, nor from the south. But God is the judge: he putteth down one, and setteth up another* [this scripture has carried me through the years of continual promotion on my job as well as in the church]

Ephesians 6:18-20 *Praying always with*

all prayer and supplication in the Spirit….And for me, that utterance may be given unto me, that I may open my mouth boldly, to make known the mystery of the gospel For which I am an ambassador in bonds: that therein I may speak boldly, as I ought to speak [this scripture continues to help me through my struggle with my voice and my hesitation to preach]

Matthew 18:18 - *Verily I say unto you, Whatsoever ye shall bind on earth shall be bound in heaven: and whatsoever ye shall loose on earth shall be loosed in heaven* [this is my fighting scripture to let the enemy know the power God has given me through Christ Jesus]

Philippians 4:13 *I can do all things through Christ which strengtheneth me.* [this is my fighting scripture to let the enemy know the power God has given me through Christ Jesus]

Isaiah 54:17 *No weapon that is formed against thee shall prosper; and every tongue that shall rise against thee in judgment thou shalt condemn. This is the heritage of the servants of the LORD, and their righteousness is of me, saith the LORD.* [this is my fighting scripture to let the enemy know the power God has given me through Christ Jesus]

Deuteronomy 28:13 *And the LORD shall make thee the head, and not the tail; and thou shalt be above only, and thou shalt not be beneath* [this scripture reminds me of who I am in Christ and gives me the boldness to reach beyond my present circumstances]

1 Corinthians 15:57 *But thanks be to God, which giveth us the victory through* *our Lord Jesus Christ.* [this is my fighting scripture to let the enemy know the power God has given me through Christ Jesus]

Deuteronomy 6:11 *And it shall be... give thee.... houses full of all good things, which thou filledst not, and wells digged, which thou diggedst not, vineyards and olive trees, which thou plantedst not; when thou shalt have eaten and be full* [this scripture reminds me of the things God promises to give me i.e. house(s), land, wealth, material possessions]

Philippians 3:13-14 *Brethren, I count not myself to have apprehended : but this one thing I do, forgetting those things which are behind, and reaching forth unto those things which are before, I press toward the mark for the prize of the high calling of God in Christ Jesus.* [this scripture reminds me to learn from the past and press forward]

Ephesians 3:20-21 *Now unto him that is able to do exceeding abundantly above all that we ask or think, according to the power that worketh in us, Unto him [be] glory* [I use this scripture at the end of a service and at the end of my prayer to remind me of His ability]

Benita Kay Hairston

Messages to Our Children

Benita Hairston is the beautiful mother of three wonderful children, Joshua, Alisha and Andre. She has eight lovely grandchildren: Dashawn, Destiny, Eve, Majne, Lilliana, Belle, Jasmine and Ari.

Benita holds an Associate's degree from Erie County Community College, a Bachelor's and Master's Degree from Shaw University in North Carolina. Benita served in the United States Air Force and has worked in federal government for over twenty-years.

Benita is the first, ever, female Chaplain at the Veteran's Hospital in Buffalo, New York.

Messages to Our Children

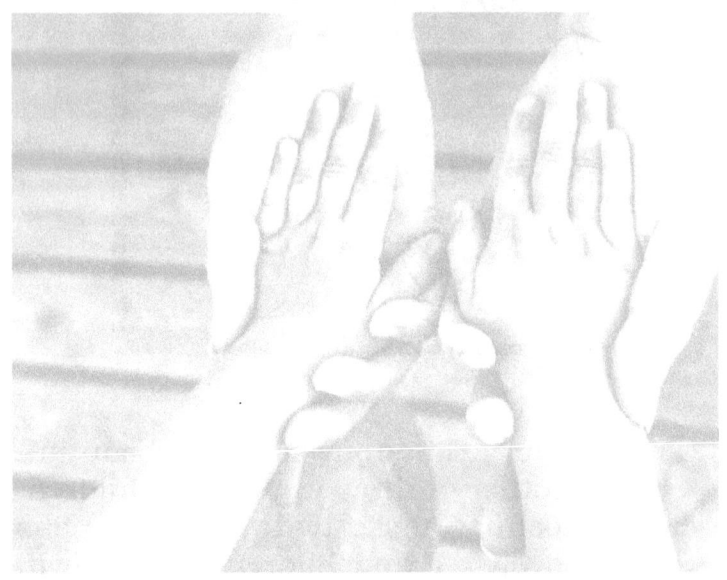

"Learn from yesterday, live for today, hope for tomorrow."

- Albert Einstein

Messages to Our Children

Tracey Morrison

Dear Tamia,

As a child, I envisioned becoming many things in life. I had so many aspirations, like to become a teacher, lawyer, Hollywood actress, a WNBA player, and to attend Duke University. (Smile), I was young then, and had so many dreams. I would tell your grandfather my career aspirations and all he would say is that you can become anything you want in life. If you want to attend Duke University, you can do it.

As children we can dream all we want, but as you get older a dream is nothing unless you take a course of action. I have always been imaginative; reading books, watching television, listening to music and stories helped expand my imagination to a new level. In addition, I enjoyed working independently and taking the initiative to work on projects because I wanted to see my ideas fulfilled.

At age 11, I began converting my ideas into paper. It was just my pencil and my thoughts communicating with one another and taking my thoughts into another dimension. It took me to a place outside my rural environment. From that day on I knew that I wanted to become a screenwriter and entrepreneur. I set my mind on fulfilling those aspirations and took a Theater Arts I and II course in high school.

During my senior year, I set my mind on moving to New York City after high school. My mother was upset that I hadn't yet to applied to college, and she told me that I needed to apply or I was going to end up at a local community college. When the opportunity presented itself to move to NYC to study business, I let fear talk me out of my dream. I decided to enroll in a four year college at North Carolina A&T State University on 1/30/2000, and received my acceptance letter in March 2000. I didn't take the time to prepare for the SAT, and due to my SAT grade I couldn't enroll in the Business program at NC A&T.

I set my mind in majoring in Theater Arts, but again, I let fear talk me out of that. I remember looking at a pamphlet from NC A&T on the list of majors, and saw the possible careers in business with a Sociology degree. I decided to major in Sociology with a concentration in Business. I went along with my career, but wasn't happy. I felt as if something was missing.

My love for writing came back to me after watching Tyler Perry's play, *Meet the Browns*. I started writing stories in between my lunch breaks, during my quiet time, during conference meetings and in my car. I wrote until that love of writing revived deep within my soul. I said to myself that fear will no longer hold me back.

I attended book club conferences, and enrolled in UCLA online screenwriting program. I'm now making a career transition to my first love. I'm pursuing a Corporate MBA degree at one of the top business schools in the country, and will start my filming business after finishing school.

Your grandfather made a career transition to become a business entrepreneur after working for the factory plant during the 1980s. He had ambitions to own an electrical company, and took a leap of faith to become that. He didn't consider the impossibility. He just knew in his heart that he wanted to become an entrepreneur. He attended community college to study electrician, where he graduated with honors in 1991. He received his business license in 1992. Your grandfather named his company after his three children, TT&T Electrical Services. Today he's a successful electrician entrepreneur throughout the Sandhills, NC regions.

With God all things are possible. Never let obstacle stopped you. Pursuing your dream is similar to driving on a one way street. The one way sign will lead you to your destination. You have control of the wheel to drive along that one way street. While driving along that one way, you may run into traffic, accidents, pot holes, reckless drivers and bad weather conditions, but, the key is to keep driving along that one way street.

It may take you a while to reach your destination, but don't turn around or else you will see the wrong way sign. Just remember that you control the wheel, and it will go where you direct it to go.

Messages to Our Children

Tracey Morrison hails from Raeford, North Carolina. She has two fantastic sisters and she is the middle child. She is the fabulous mother of a wonderful daughter, Tamia Morrison, the aunt of one nephew, Deontae Baldwin and god mother of Jada Hines-Bease.

Tracey grew up in a working middle class family (mother-Social Worker, father- self-employed electrician). She graduated in 2000 from Hoke County High School in Raeford, NC.

Tracey received a Bachelor's of Art degree in Sociology with a concentration in Business Administration in 2004 from NC A&T State University - Greensboro, NC.
She is a Graduate student at Florida International University online - Miami, FL pursuing a Corporate MBA degree.

Tracey has been employed in County Government for more than five years. She is pursuing a career transition to become a screenwriter. Tracey has taken an online screenwriting class at UCLA. She admires the works of Tyler Perry, David E. Talbert, Angela Basset, Oprah Winfrey, TD Jakes, and Spike Lee.

Tracey's personal interests/hobbies include: meditating, God, family, friends, inspirational quotes, movies, writing, reading books, art, African American history, traveling, poems, encouraging people, exercise and a healthy lifestyle.

Messages to Our Children

Messages to Our Children

"The more that you read, the more things you will know. The more you learn the more places you'll go!"

- Dr. Seuss

Messages to Our Children

Brenda L. Brooks

We Are Family

We are one family. We are a unity of CHRIST. We are united by mothers, fathers, great and grandparents. GOD is the head of our family. So to Him we owe our praise, love, honor and glory. To our parents we owe our thanks, devotion, respect and love, and to each other we owe peace, kindness, love, and respect. WE ARE THE FAMILY and we owe to ourselves self-respect, endurance, self-control, diligence, honor and truth.

God made us a family, so let's preserve it and honor His Words "Love thy neighbor as thyselves, Love one another, and Love thy God first and foremost. Love the Lord thy God with all thy heart and soul..." We are GOD's children and GOD's family. Let us preserve the White/Lee family. "We are family"

Friends

My Friend, your friend, our friend, their friend, nobody's friend, who is it?

Who is your friend? Who is not your friend? What determines what a friend is? Do you really have to like the person who you call your friend?

A friend is a trustworthy person whom you can share stories, secrets, time, laughter, tears or even a meal at home or not.

A friend should be someone who wouldn't betray you, someone who wouldn't steal from you, your money or your significant other. They would not hurt you at all.

You should trust your friend to be

honest, loving, caring, and faithful no matter what. The tenderness of friendship is heartfelt, intimate and touching feelings.

My friend should be all of the above, a good friend always, and a true friend to the end, a best friend through thick and thin until the end.

I can't call a person a friend if they talk about you or me behind our back, back stab you for another friend, steal from you, your money or possessions and lie to your face. Grin in your face, all the time while deceiving you is a no no.

Why does the word "friend" come out of the mouth of someone who deliberately deceives back-stab, lie or steal from you? They are not your friend. You can't trust them and you simply cannot believe a word that they say. You lose respect for that person and you do not want them in your life.

Messages to Our Children

Do you still like them after all they do to deceive you? Get a grip, so lose them say bye-bye. Move on; try another person under a microscope before you let them into your life.

Life itself is a lesson to learn. All the teachings given by parents, grandparents or elders only tell you of something that they had to say to appease them by saying this is what I have learned, what I was told, or what I believed. The life that they led either came from advice or what they decided they wanted to do regardless of "maybe" sound advice given but they may say "what do they know about me, I'm a different person then they are".

No one lives someone else's life. No two lives are the same so who do you learn from, yourself or the other so called "smart" people who are telling you this or that?

Life lessons have many titles for

Messages to Our Children

example respect, love, happiness, friendship, pride, and your purpose.

First of all, respect is not a question of if, why, when, or how. Respect is truth. Respect is what is desired from a person. Respect should be taught at birth. How? When a baby cries for attention they are either told to stop crying or given a look of disapproval. They then learn to understand and respect their parents' wishes.

Correcting behavior by using please and thank you teaches that it is a proper way to show respect. You teach to have manners by saying I'm sorry, pardon me, excuse me, please and thank you. To some people this is old fashion. You learn to give respect and also desire respect from others.

The best of life you get is from love. You get heartfelt nurturing through love. Love gives you a feeling of being appreciated, admired and cared for. A parent gives children love when they show them that *I love you* smile, hug or praise. A child grows well knowing that they are loved.

There are children that never get their love from their parents and sometimes in their lives they grow bitter and not give love to anyone else. They get in relationship after relationship and never learn to love. Therefore, they are not able to accept love. It is important, therefore, to let children know that they are loved by actions and words. A kiss helps them to really feel loved.

Happiness is very necessary in a person's life. You just cannot live without some happiness. When you are happy, you live a better life. Things work on your behalf because people see you as a happy being and they can to communicate better with you, enjoy you, and even love you.

Messages to Our Children

You could just laugh a little, smile, talk with a gleeful voice, or just whistle while you work. You can chase the blues away with happiness and receive and keep friends.

Friends are important in your life. You have a person to consult you, interact with, enjoy and have fun with. Friends, some in more than one way, can be a good friend, a buddy, or a best friend. Each can play a great part in your life, but you should choose friends wisely.

Take pride in yourself. Be a person of good character; be charming in your personality. Do excel and master what you do. Give attention to yourself by good personal grooming, proper speaking and politeness. It is noticeable how much you care about yourself by the pride you have for yourself. Be proud, be understanding, and have a high expectation for your life. A low self-esteem takes away how you feel

Messages to Our Children

and pulls you down.

Be proud of whom you are, how you look, where you come from, and let pride be in your speech and presence. You have a lot to be proud of in your life. You have accomplishments, dignity and love for yourself. So acclaim who you are with pride and dignity.

Life has given you a purpose. You have a purpose for being born; your walk of life has a purpose. Your being as a person, a human has a purpose. You were born with predestment for your life and someone else's life. Where you were born, to whom you were born from has an ultimate purpose.

The time is set, the purpose is set, your walk is set and the purpose is part of your destiny and it was set. You have a predestined future, also a life which has every dream fulfilled, but it cannot happen unless you figure it out. Only after you have figured it out will the things predestined for your purpose happen and you will be free to act upon it.

Life's lesson isn't always easy, but they are necessary. When you were given life it was to be relished and enjoyed, but taken seriously.

Who you are in life puts a stamp of approval on another's life. You have to take it like a grain of salt. Be mindful of too much nonsense and less attention given to the unimportant things in life.

Messages to Our Children

Messages to Our Children

Brenda Brooks is a native of Alexandria, VA. She is the spectacular wife of Theodore Brooks and together they have three dynamic sons, one beautiful daughter, ten grandsons, two granddaughters, two great grandsons and one great granddaughter.

They are the "T" family. She named all of her children with names starting with "T" and the tradition has been passed down to the grandchildren and now great grandchildren.

Brenda attended DC Public Schools starting at the age of 12. She went on to earn a Bachelor of Arts in Advertising Art and Art Education from the University of the District of Columbia. She is certified in Theological Ministry and Pastoral Care.

Brenda retired from the DC Public Schools System. After retiring, she has been trying to relax and let God inspire her to a higher calling.

She spent several years working in Civil Service and for the Department of Agriculture.

Brenda's hobbies:
She still paints occasionally and writes poetry and inspirational reflections and stories. She is a member of Meade Memorial Episcopal Church Gospel Truth Choir, Alter Guild, Lay Reader, and Breakfast Club Committee. She spends some of her free time making quilts for the family. Each year she uses a new theme for family unity.

She desires to travel around the world. Her most recent trip has been to Miami, Florida, and a few years ago to South Africa with the Tutu family on a pilgrimage. She visited Senegal, Ghana, Ivory Coast, and New Guam.

Messages to Our Children

Messages to Our Children

*"Don't walk behind me; I may not lead.
Don't walk in front of me; I may not follow.
Just walk beside me and be my friend."*
                                        -Albert Camus

Messages to Our Children

Towanna L. Thomas

Giving birth to my two sons was the most amazing experience I endured. I had many doubts in my ability to be a parent but I have been proven wrong. I thank God every day for giving me the ability to use the gift of birth to raise them to be the men they are today. Given the opportunity to be a parent is the most valuable and meaningful experience received from God. With hard work and trial and error, I was able to be the loving and caring mother I have become.

My advice to my sons and generations to follow is to enjoy life to its fullest! Take advantage of the opportunities set before you. Pay attention to what's being taught, observe what's being done and expect to be better. As a parent, my job is to teach you to the best of my ability expose you to as many opportunities as possible and push you to your limit to exceed, excel, and succeed.

By doing this, I first have to teach you about God! A life plan has already been set for us by God, so my job is to follow his plan to the best of my ability. As you were growing, I always read books to you and bible stories were one of many I read to you.

Next, I had to teach you about values, respect, love, honesty, and integrity. Have a plan, set goals and try to stick by them. When obstacles get in your way, figure out how to maneuver around them. Take chances and be willing to step out of the box. A higher education is important in being successful but most importantly is to finish what you start.

I also have some quotes I like to live by:

Messages to Our Children

-First God, self, family, friends and others. Treat everyone with respect.

-Give 110% in whatever you do. Go the extra mile and don't expect anything in return.

-Lead by example

-Live, laugh, love.

-Love they neighbor

-Do unto others as you have them do unto you.

-Don't let anyone tell you what you cannot do.

-Don't let fear be your reason for not doing something.

-If at first you don't succeed, try, try, again.

-Hard work and dedication will pay off in the end.

-Sometimes you have to swim upstream.

- Be a leader, not a follower.

-Love God, self, family, friends, and others.

-make wise choices and try not to have any regrets. Use it as a learning experience.
-Don't rush life. Enjoy the moment and take one day at a time.

I love my family and I want to thank God for them all! My parents gave me the greatest childhood and I hope I was able to do the same for my children. Memories and stories has been set and pasted down and we know history repeats itself. I remember as a child how I thought I had all the answers and I didn't want to take my parents advice at times. Well, I wished I did and I didn't realize they were giving the advice from their experiences and wanted to best for me.

By passing on the advice, it was in the hopes of making life easier. To save you all some trouble, please, please, please, learn and listen to the old and wise. It's nothing like saying "I wish I had listened". We can't go back and relive the past. If I could pass on one last message to my children, it would be to trust in God, follow your dreams and don't let anyone stop you.

Messages to Our Children

Towanna "Tina" Thomas has been married to her wonderful husband Duane Thomas for over twenty-five years. He is a retired Army soldier. Their first duty station as husband and wife was Aschaffenburg, Germany. They relocated back to their hometown upon retirement. Tina enjoyed the life of a military wife!! She continues to give back to the Army. She is proud of the motto "Be All You Can Be, Go Army and Army Strong!"

Tina is the mother of two handsome sons Duane and Durell and the grandmother of one equally handsome grandson. She is a native of Washington, D.C. and has three strong and protective brothers. She is the only girl in the family and loves it that way! Tina is a member of the "T" family. Her mother named all of her children with names starting with "T" and the tradition has been passed down to the grandchildren and now great grandchildren.

Tina attended the D.C. public school system and went on to earn her Bachelor of Art degree in Theater Arts from the University of the District of Columbia. Tina studied dance to include ballet, tap, jazz, modern, and ballroom dance.
She participated in the marching band as a Pom Pom girl in high school and college.

Tina has been employed with the Federal Government for over twenty-five years. Her professional career started in Aschaffenburg, GE in the Personnel and Human Resources field.

Tina's hobbies include: Dancing, exercising, reading, cooking, and spending time with family. She is a Volunteer and Usher for the Breakfast Committee at Meade Memorial Episcopal Church

Messages to Our Children

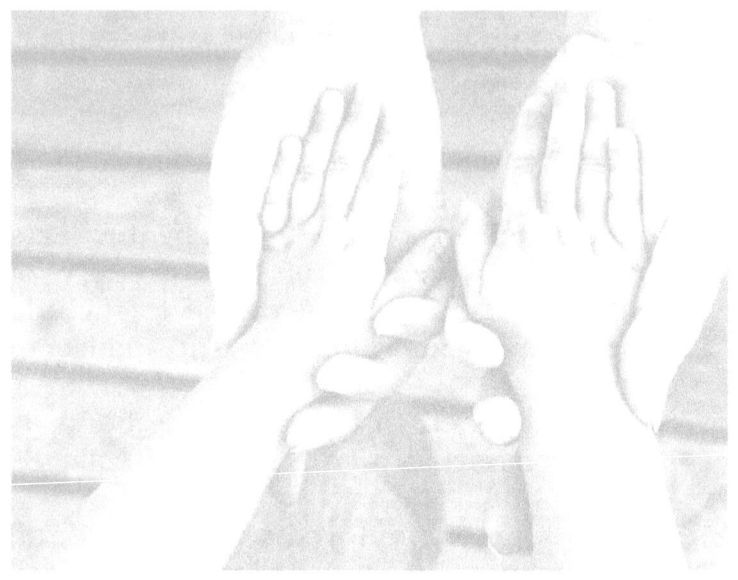

"Others have seen what is and asked why; I have seen what could be and asked why not."

-Pablo Picasso

Messages to Our Children

Valencia Warren-Gibbs

In honor of my mother Lillian Lee Warren, who taught directly and indirectly is her family tree. Her favorite phrase was "Keep on livin'". Living through experiences becomes the best teacher. When you ask yourself "why", ask "why not". Everything that you experience is preparing you for an event, season, and reason. Do your best; treat others in the way you want to be treated. The caveat is to pay attention to the way others treat you.

When you receive treatment from someone that is less than desirable, do not go against your morals to reciprocate. Instead, respond with grace, bow out gracefully, and retreat. Do not lose focus of the big picture, which encompasses your dream that is already been dreamt for you. There is nothing more nurturing than a mother's love. "Mothering" is not lessons through an academic curriculum at any university and college. "Mothering" is the description of a woman whose love endures from inception to eternity, which is a full perfect imperfection.

Parenting is not what makes her great, it is her willingness to teach us, "learning to be great" in adversity through the grace of "God". Thank you, God, for this mother who fits in this description "Lillian Lee".

Messages to Our Children

Dr. Valencia Warren-Gibbs (ABD) is the dynamic wife to Michael R. Gibbs and mother to Xavier Dunkley, Malcolm Dunkley, and Jade (Lillian) Gibbs. She is a native to the City of Detroit, love chess, reading, new interest in golf, and value family and friendship.

Valencia is a 20 year career accounting professional that has ventured into entrepreneurship in the trucking transportation industry "Network Logistical Solutions, LLC" d.b.a NLS (a joint-venture with Network Towing Inc.). Her goal is to create an organization that empowers others to do for others and achieve their desires.

Valencia believes the antidotes to heal pain is to Live despite all, love anyway, and laugh often as hard as you can .

Messages to Our Children

What she does know: "You do not have to perfect, but you do have to be "present" to be a gift to the world." Her goal is to leave an imprint of positive change in the lives that I seek to empower; for generations.

Messages to Our Children

Messages to Our Children

"The most common way people give up their power is by thinking they don't have any."

- Alice Walker

Messages to Our Children

Alberta Lampkins

December 1, 2013

> *As I sit here gazing out the kitchen window, my heart is filled with wonder as I observe a little black bird flying free. I wonder how long it took that bird to become strong enough to fly.*

To my daughter Alexis, my son Ahmad, my grandson Elijah, my nieces, my nephews, and my future grandchildren and to all the children connected to this story, You Are a Perfect Gift. God picked you to be exactly who you are. There is no one else in this world like you. From the moment you were formed, to the moment

Messages to Our Children

you made your presence in this world, God has shaped you and molded you to be unquestionably who you are.

There is a wonderful plan for your life and my prayer is that you will find your purpose and accomplish everything that you set out to do in this time. Know that you are destined to be great in God's eyes. Each of you has your own set of treasures and strengths within you. The strengths that God gives you are not like any others. So seek to find yours, and when you do, build upon those strengths and push towards success.

Some of my greatest strengths are my love of learning, my hope and optimism. I expect the best for you in the future and I pray you work hard to achieve it. You can be as creative as you want to be, so show the world who you are!

I have been blessed to be surrounded by great people in my life. I've

Messages to Our Children

learned that it is important and wise to listen to those people in your existence who gives you good guidance. Take heed to their messages, for good guidance is invaluable. And, to the people who want to change you, to stop you from following your dreams, to stop you from reaching your goals, to hurt you or to bring negativity in your life, let them go. Your life is too important and heart is too precious.

There will be some hard days, some tough days and some sad days. However, remember this; for every one of those kinds of days, God will give you good days, great days and some absolutely wonderful days. Each day is a new beginning and presents a new opportunity to change something, do something and be something great.

Life is an amazing journey, especially if you learn to seek peace, joy, love and happiness within you. The highest form of freedom is to know who you are. You are beautiful, you are wonderful and YOU ARE LOVED.

Don't hurry life. Just as it takes a small bird time to build its wings and become strong enough to fly, so does it take time to build who you are meant to be. Look for the messages from above and from those who love you to help guide you along the way. Never give up. Know that whether I am here or gone, you have someone in your corner routing you on.

If there was one thing that I could leave with each one of you and each person reading this message, it would be to leave you my smile. My smile is probably the greatest gift that God has given me. His light shines through my smile and I pass it on to you. May you always know that you are loved.

I honor my parents, Sam and

Messages to Our Children

Macieon Hairston and my aunt Alberta Lettie Martin by passing on hope, love, peace and joy to each one of you.

Unity

I heard a beautiful song today,
The words wrapped around my soul,
Like the beat of an
Ancient drum roll.

The melody swayed me, as the song
romanced my ears and lifted my spirit.
It was like gentle waves of the
Caribbean Sea
Or shade from a beautiful oak tree.

As the beat bounced closer, the
rhythm stole my heart.

It was the voices of families.
With words of love, peace and
harmony.
Family
Singing of pride and strength in
unity
Voices of all people joined together
as one
In hope of success for the many of
those to come.

-Alberta Lampkins

Messages to Our Children

Messages to Our Children

Alberta Lampkins is a proud Army wife and has been married to her husband Al for more than twenty-five years. She is the mother of two awesome children, Alexis and Ahmad and the grandmother of a handsome grandson, Elijah, whom she believes is the best grandson in the world.

Alberta is a very passionate and dedicated advocate for children and adults. She has worked in both Child Protective Services and Adult Services. She is the project coordinator for *Messages to Our Children* and the author of the book, *Teach Me How to Fly*.

Alberta holds a Bachelor of Arts and a Master of Arts Degree in Sociology from Fayetteville State University. She is the founder and Publisher of A.L. Savvy Publications established in 2014.

Messages to Our Children

"One thing alone I charge you. As you live, believe in life! Always human beings will live and progress to greater, broader and fuller life. The only possible death is to lose belief in this truth."

-W.E.B. Dubois

Messages to Our Children

May you find all these treasures in life!

```
G S R H T U S M W G P
V S P I H S D N E I R F
L E C A E P N U H A K W
J C I O H T I A F G B M
T C Z T R J O S K X W N
Q U E X P G F V L X X L
N S P K I N D N E S S O
E V O L U R C Y B R P J
P P H B L W O N H X B S
L Q S D A J C A M T A Y
H A P P I N E S S C T U
H H Y T I V I T A E R C
```

Creativity
Faith
Friendship
Happiness
Hope

Joy
Kindness
Love
Peace
Success

Messages to Our Children

Messages to Our Children

Add a Message to a child connected to you and pass it on.

To: _____

From: _____

Date: _____

Message:

_____
_____
_____
_____
_____
_____
_____
_____
_____
_____
_____
_____
_____
_____
_____

Messages to Our Children

Messages to Our Children

Messages to Our Children

Messages to Our Children

Complete your family tree

Messages to Our Children

Messages to Our Children

Complete your family tree

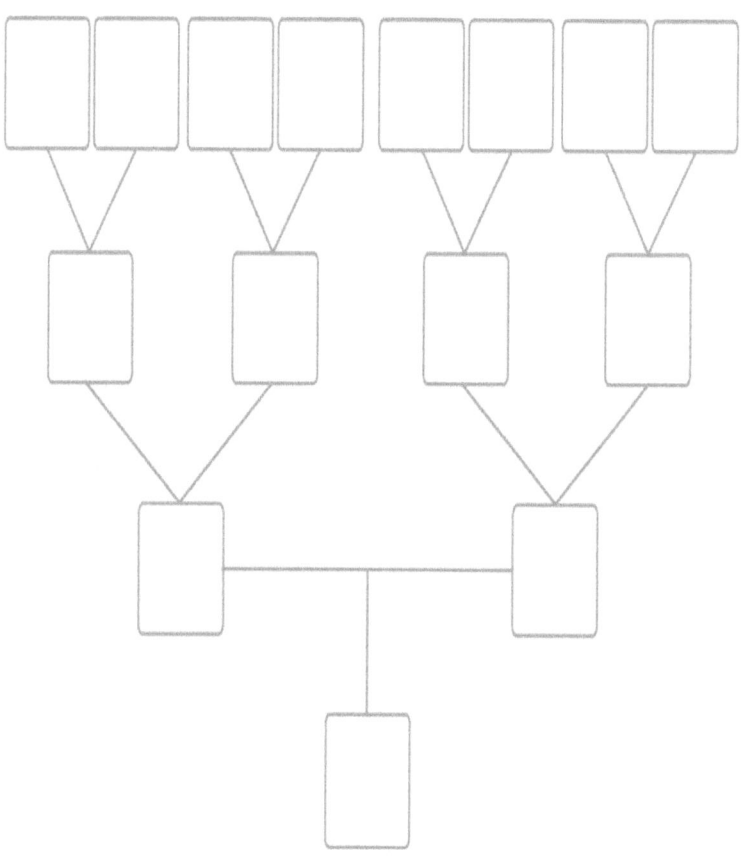

Messages to Our Children

ABOUT THE AUTHOR

Alberta Lampkins is a proud Army wife and has been married to her husband CSM Al Lampkins for over twenty-five years. She is the mother of two awesome children, Alexis and Ahmad and the grandmother of a handsome grandson, Elijah, whom she believes is the best grandson in the world.

Alberta is the Project Coordinator for *Messages to Our Children* and the author of the book, *Teach Me How to Fly*.

Alberta holds a Bachelor of Arts and a Master of Arts Degree in Sociology from Fayetteville State University. Alberta founded A.L. Savvy Publications, an independent publishing company, after realizing how much she enjoyed listening and reading stories about everyday people. She wanted to create a platform for others to share their stories in print.

Alberta is a native of Buffalo, New York, however, currently resides in Tennessee with her husband and their son.

Visit Alberta at:
Facebook.com/A.L.SavvyPublications.
Twitter.com/ALSavvyPub or on the web
http://alsavvypublications.com.

Messages to Our Children

Messages to Our Children

www.ingramcontent.com/pod-product-compliance
Lightning Source LLC
Chambersburg PA
CBHW031417290426
44110CB00011B/426